# ANTS

*by Josh Gregory*

**Children's Press®**

An Imprint of Scholastic Inc.

Content Consultant
Dr. Stephen S. Ditchkoff
Professor of Wildlife Ecology and Management
Auburn University
Auburn, Alabama

Photographs ©: cover: Sergey Bezberdy/Caters News Service; 1: Pascal Goetgheluck/Science Source; 2: inkwelldodo/Shutterstock, Inc.; 3: inkwelldodo/Shutterstock, Inc.; 4: NaturePL/Superstock, Inc.; 5 background: NaturePL/Superstock, Inc.; 5 top inset: Pushish Images/Shutterstock, Inc.; 5 bottom inset: Lisa und Wilfried Bahnmaller/Media Bakery; 7: Leonid Serebrennikov/Superstock, Inc.; 8: Pushish Images/Shutterstock, Inc.; 11: Pascal Goetgheluck/Science Source; 12: Mitsuhiko Imamori/Minden Pictures/National Geographic Creative; 15: National Geographic Creative/Alamy Images; 16: Minden Pictures/Superstock, Inc.; 19: Yon Marsh Natural History/Alamy Images; 20: Encyclopaedia Britannica/UIG/Getty Images; 23: Lefteris Papaulakis/Shutterstock, Inc.; 24: inkwelldodo/Shutterstock, Inc.; 27: NaturePL/Superstock, Inc.; 28: Minden Pictures/Superstock, Inc.; 31: The Natural History Museum/Alamy Images; 32: juniors/Superstock, Inc.; 35: Minden Pictures/Superstock, Inc.; 36: LucBrousseau/iStockphoto/Thinkstock; 39: Stephen Belcher/Minden Pictures; 40: Lisa und Wilfried Bahnmaller/Media Bakery; 44 background: inkwelldodo/Shutterstock, Inc.; 45 background: inkwelldodo/Shutterstock, Inc.; 46: Pascal Goetgheluck/Science Source.

Maps by Bob Italiano.

Library of Congress Cataloging-in-Publication Data
Names: Gregory, Josh, author.
Title: Ants / by Josh Gregory.
Other titles: Nature's children (New York, N.Y.)
Description: New York : Children's Press, an imprint of Scholastic Inc.,
   [2017] | Series: Nature's children
Identifiers: LCCN 2015043532| ISBN 9780531230268 (library binding : alk. paper) | ISBN 9780531219324 (pbk. : alk. paper)
Subjects: LCSH: Ants—Juvenile literature.
Classification: LCC QL568.F7 G722 | DDC 595.79/6—dc23
LC record available at http://lccn.loc.gov/2015043532

Printed in China 62
SCHOLASTIC, CHILDREN'S PRESS, and associated logos are trademarks and/or registered trademarks of Scholastic Inc.

1 2 3 4 5 6 7 8 9 10 R 26 25 24 23 22 21 20 19 18 17

# Ants

| | |
|---|---|
| **Class** | Insecta |
| **Order** | Hymenoptera |
| **Family** | Formicidae |
| **Genus** | 283 genera |
| **Species** | Around 12,000 species |
| **World distribution** | Worldwide, except for Antarctica, Greenland, Iceland, and certain islands |
| **Habitat** | Almost all land habitats |
| **Distinctive physical characteristics** | Range in length from 0.04 to 1.18 inches (1 to 30 millimeters); usually black, brown, red, or yellow; body segmented into head, thorax, and abdomen; thorax and abdomen connected by very narrow waist; antennae bent into elbow shape; two sets of jaws; males and queens have wings, while workers do not |
| **Habits** | Live in enormous family groups called colonies; most species build elaborate underground homes with many tunnels and chambers; strict social structure with three classes: queens, workers, and males; communicate mainly through scent and touch; defend home against predators by biting or stinging |
| **Diet** | Varies greatly between species; some eat plants; others eat fungi; some are even carnivorous |

# Contents

## CHAPTER 1

# Ants Everywhere!

Imagine waking up one morning to find hundreds of tiny black ants crawling around your kitchen. Your first instinct might be to start smashing them or spraying them with ant killer. But if you take a closer look instead, you could find something amazing.

You might notice a line of ants between the kitchen cabinets where food is stored and a crack where the floor meets the wall. If you followed this line outside, it might lead you to some small, black mounds of soil. Huge numbers of ants could be crawling around these hills. These numbers are nothing, however, compared to what lies below. Underground, thousands upon thousands of ants are hard at work performing the tasks their society relies upon. Some build tunnels. Others care for young. Many are carefully storing the food they have taken from your kitchen. It is an entire city of **insects** living beneath your backyard!

*A line of black garden ants marches along a path through moss.*

# All over the World

Ants are some of the most amazing animals on Earth. Like humans, they form complex societies. Every member plays an important role in the lives of others. Ants are also very intelligent. They can solve a variety of problems by working together. As a result, these insects have fascinated people for a very long time.

Ants can be found on almost every part of land on the planet. They are especially common in habitats with hot weather, such as rain forests. The only areas that lack ants are Antarctica, Greenland, Iceland, and certain islands.

Ants are among the world's most common animals. In habitats such as the Amazon rain forest, there can be up to eight million ants living on every 2.5 acres (1 hectare) of land.

**FUN FACT!** The study of ants is called myrmecology.

*Weaver ants work together to weave leaves into a nest in the rain forest.*

# Small Wonders

One reason so many ants can live in one area is their small size. The smallest species is just 0.04 to 0.08 inches (1 to 2 millimeters) long. Even the largest ants only grow to lengths of about 1.18 inches (30 mm).

Ants are generally black, red, yellow, or brown. As with all insects, their bodies are divided into three main sections. These are called the head, the thorax, and the abdomen. A very skinny waist connects the thorax and abdomen. An ant's head is equipped with two separate sets of jaws: an inner set and an outer set. The ant uses the inner set to chew food. It uses the outer set to grip and carry objects. An ant also has a pair of antennae on its head. Each antenna has a single bend in it, making it appear similar to an elbow.

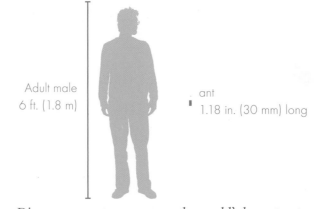

Adult male
6 ft. (1.8 m)

ant
1.18 in. (30 mm) long

*Dinoponera ants are among the world's largest ants.*

## CHAPTER 2

# An Ant's Life

Ants live together in huge societies called colonies. A single colony may contain anywhere from thousands to millions of members. For such a large society to be successful, each ant must play a role that benefits the community. Unlike many animals, an ant is more concerned about the success of its colony than about its own, individual survival. Ants focus on making sure their relatives have food and shelter and are able to continue reproducing. They will do whatever it takes to succeed at this.

There are three classes of ants in every colony. These are queen ants, male ants, and worker ants. Each class has a very different appearance and lifestyle. Additionally, the ants play different yet equally important roles in their society. No ant colony can last long if it is missing any one of the three classes.

**FUN FACT!** All worker ants are female. However, they are unable to mate.

*Among honeypot ants, certain workers store food in their bodies so it can later be released to feed other ants in the colony.*

# The Three Classes

Queen ants are almost entirely devoted to a single activity: laying eggs. A queen might lay as many as one million eggs over the course of her life. Amazingly, this life can last several decades, which is very uncommon for an insect. Queens are much larger than other classes of ants, and they are born with a pair of wings. In some ant species, there is one queen for each colony. In others, there are several queens per colony.

Like queens, male ants have one main job. Once they reach adulthood, they generally mate with a queen and then die shortly afterward. Males are larger than worker ants, yet smaller than queens, and they have wings.

Worker ants are the kind you are likely to see in your home or yard. They are smaller than the other two classes and do not have wings. They are responsible for keeping a colony running smoothly. This includes everything from digging tunnels to gathering food to caring for young.

*A queen ant in Peru prepares to take flight.*

# From Eggs to Adults

To understand the unique way ants live, it is necessary to learn about their complex life cycle. There are four main stages in an ant's development. These are the egg, the larva, the pupa, and the adult. A queen ant lays eggs soon after she mates with a male. A group of worker ants then takes over the eggs and cares for them. Eventually, the eggs hatch into larvae.

An ant larva looks like a tiny worm. It does not have legs or eyes. Worker ants bring food to larvae. This helps the larvae grow quickly. As they get bigger, they molt several times. Eventually, they reach the pupa stage.

A pupa looks somewhat like a fully grown ant. However, it is lighter in color, and its legs stay folded up close to its body. Some species live inside cocoons during this stage. Others do not. Eventually, the pupa hatches into its final adult form.

*Certain worker ants are in charge of feeding and caring for the colony's larvae.*

# Creating a New Colony

An ant's class is determined by how much food workers feed it when it is a pupa. When the colony decides it needs more queens, it simply chooses pupae to be fed more food. One reason it might do this is to establish new colonies. In some species, a queen and some males fly away from the colony to mate. After mating, the queen might fly away and dig a small hole. There, she removes her wings and lays her eggs. These eggs become the new colony's first workers after they hatch. From there, the colony continues growing.

Not all ants begin their colonies the same way. In some species, workers start a new colony by carrying eggs to a new location. They raise one of these eggs to be a queen, and the colony grows from there. In other cases, a new queen might mate in her home colony. Then she travels to the location of a new colony accompanied by a team of workers.

*Black garden worker ants help a queen and males prepare to fly away and mate.*

## CHAPTER 3

# Life in the Colony

An ant colony is not just a huge, swarming mass of insects. In fact, a colony's underground home isn't all that different from a human city. Ants build a variety of structures below the earth's surface. Each structure has an important purpose for the colony. Chambers and tunnels are arranged as carefully as the roads and buildings in a human town. There are rooms set aside for workers to care for eggs and larvae. There are also food storage chambers. Queen ants usually have their own chambers for mating and laying eggs. Other rooms are set aside for worker ants to rest when they aren't busy with other tasks.

These underground rooms are connected by a complex system of tunnels. Some tunnels are wide and travel straight through the busiest parts of a colony. These tunnels act as "highways" for the ants to travel along. Other tunnels are smaller. They split off from the main paths and lead to individual chambers.

*Many ant species build large hills above their underground tunnels and rooms.*

# Colony Construction

Ants dig by using their jaws to carry soil and other materials to the surface from underground. They work together in large numbers to quickly clear out big rooms and long tunnels. The largest ant colonies can extend more than 20 feet (6 meters) below the surface. Some also spread out 20 feet (6 m) or more in every direction.

Ants design their colonies to control the flow of air in and out of the tunnels and chambers. They do this by constructing small shafts leading to the surface. At the holes on the surface, the ants arrange dirt to shape vents that regulate the airflow. This helps control the temperature of the colony's rooms and tunnels.

Not all ant species build the same kinds of colonies. Carpenter ants make their homes by burrowing into trees and wooden structures. Army ants do not have permanent homes. The colony keeps moving, usually stopping only for the queen to lay her eggs. Workers carry larvae with them as they travel.

*Ants carry dirt out of the ground as they dig tunnels.*

# Diverse Diets

An ant's diet depends on its species and habitat. Some species mainly eat leaves. Others eat fruit, seeds, and other plant materials. Some ants prey on less powerful ants and their eggs. Army ants swarm and eat spiders, beetles, and many other animals. They have even been known to attack birds and lizards.

Instead of simply seeking out a meal when they are hungry, many ants maintain stores of food. Workers leave the colony to gather food and bring it back to special storage rooms. All the ants in the colony share these food supplies.

Many ants even grow their own food, much like humans raise crops and livestock. Some ants set aside special chambers where fungus can grow. They can then harvest the fungus to eat. Other ants eat a substance called honeydew. Insects called aphids produce this sweet liquid. The ants herd groups of aphids. When the ants are hungry, they rub the aphids to "milk" the honeydew from their bodies. The ants protect their food supply, making sure the aphids stay safe and healthy.

*Ants may herd large groups of aphids.*

# Staying in Touch

Ants rely heavily on their fellow colony members for survival. As a result, it is very important that they are able to communicate effectively. The main way they do this is by producing chemicals. Ants smell these chemicals to learn the information they need to carry out team efforts. For example, some types of ants send out scouts to find food. Once one of these ants comes across a good source of food, it creates a scent trail leading back to the colony. Other workers can follow this trail. Large numbers of them can then travel back and forth carrying pieces of food to the colony. This is why you might find a line of ants leading from your kitchen to your yard, if they get into your house.

Ants have other ways of interacting with one another, too. Sometimes they rub each other's antennae or touch each other's heads. Certain species produce sounds by rubbing their legs on their bodies.

*Leaf-cutter ants carry bits of leaves back to their colony.*

# Dealing with Threats

Because they are available in such large numbers, ants are a common food source for many animals. Some **predators** include birds, spiders, and even other ants. Anteaters are especially well suited to feasting on these insects. They use their long claws to dig into colonies. Then they stick their long snouts inside and lick up large numbers of ants all at once with their long tongues.

Ants rely on teamwork to defend their colony from threats. A single ant can rarely cause much damage on its own. A big enough group, however, can defend itself against even large animals. Ants are fearless when defending their homes. They never back down from a fight and are willing to sacrifice themselves for the good of the colony. They crawl all over an invader's body and bite down with their sharp jaws. Some species also have stingers at the tip of their abdomen.

*A group of ants attacks a tiger moth in Vietnam.*

## CHAPTER 4

# Incredible Insects

So far, scientists have discovered about 12,000 different species of ants living today. However, there might be many more. In fact, some experts estimate that we have found only about half of the world's current ant species. Part of the reason for this is that ants often live underground and out of sight. In addition, many species might live in remote areas where scientists cannot easily travel. Despite these difficulties, experts are always working hard to discover new ant species.

The earliest ant species probably appeared somewhere between 168 million and 140 million years ago. At first, they were not as common a sight as they are today. However, around 100 million years ago, more varieties of plants began to appear. This gave ancient ants new foods to eat and places to live. Over time, different ant species developed abilities and lifestyles that suited their many different habitats. This eventually resulted in the thousands of ant species living today.

*Researchers have found prehistoric ants in amber,*
*the hardened remains of ancient tree sap.*

# Bees and Wasps

The world's many insect species are divided into groups called orders. Ants belong to the order called Hymenoptera. Along with ants, this order includes bees, wasps, and other similar insects. At first glance, a bee or a wasp might not seem very similar to an ant. However, these insects actually have quite a bit in common. For example, they all have an extremely narrow waist between their thorax and abdomen.

Like ants, many other Hymenopterans also live in huge colonies. Bees often construct homes called hives, and many types of wasps build large nests. Though some Hymenopterans lead fairly solitary lives, many have complex social structures just as ants do. Some bee species, such as honeybees and bumblebees, have a three-class social system that is very similar to that of ants. There are queen bees, worker bees, and male bees called drones.

*Some bees build their hives out of wax.*

# Similar Yet Different

When many people think of ants, they are reminded of a group of insects called termites. Ants and termites are not actually very close relatives. Termites belong to a separate order called Blattodea. However, it is easy to see why people might think these two kinds of insects are related. They look a lot alike, they are found in many of the same places, and they lead somewhat similar lifestyles. As a result, they are commonly mistaken for each other.

One of the main physical differences between ants and termites is that termites lack a Hymenopteran's thin waist. They are also usually a lighter color than most ant species.

Like ants, termites live in colonies and build enormous homes. Sometimes they dig underground or into tree stumps or logs. Other times, they build huge mounds out of dirt. In places where humans live, they often chew their way into wooden buildings. This makes them a major pest for many people.

*There are nearly 3,000 known species of termites.*

## CHAPTER 5

# Helpful or Harmful?

Because ants are so common, many species have habitats that overlap with the places where humans live. Unfortunately, ants are not always the best neighbors. In going about their everyday lives, ants can cause many problems for people.

In wild habitats, carpenter ants build their colonies by burrowing into logs and stumps. But in places where people live, they chew their way into the walls of buildings. This can cause major damage. Other ant species can ruin crops by gnawing off leaves. Some are even known to infest electronic equipment.

Even when ants aren't damaging anything, they can be a nuisance. Once they make their way into a kitchen, it can be difficult to get rid of them. In addition, some species have painful bites and stings that can harm people they attack.

*Ants may invade a home in huge numbers, causing a lot of damage.*

# Affecting the Environment

Ants can also cause problems in wild areas. As people travel and ship goods around the world, they sometimes bring new species to places where they do not naturally belong. When a new species is introduced to an area, it can throw off the natural balance of the ecosystem. Introduced ant species might take up too much space, forcing other insects away. If there is nothing that can prey on them, their population might grow too quickly. The ants might also take over food sources that native species rely on.

One particularly troublesome introduced species is the yellow crazy ant. Its native origins are uncertain. Experts do know that these ants are not native to the North American and Australian habitats they have invaded. Yellow crazy ants have caused other types of ants to become less common in these places. On one Australian island, they have also reduced the crab population by killing them and taking over their homes.

*Yellow crazy ants have damaged native species on Australia's Christmas Island.*

# Positive Effects

Even though ants can be troublesome, they are not completely bad. In fact, ants play many important roles in keeping the environment healthy. For example, their tunneling helps water and air travel deep underground. This improves the quality of the soil and makes it easier for plants to grow. Ants also assist plants by helping to spread their seeds. As they carry fruit and other plant parts to their colonies for food, seeds can fall all around the area. These seeds grow into new plants.

Ants are also an important food source. Without them, many animals would starve. And as ants prey on plants and animals, they help keep the populations of those species from growing out of control. It is all part of a delicate natural balance.

Ants are fascinating animals. Though people have studied them closely for many years, we still have a lot to learn about them. These incredible insects hold many secrets yet to be discovered.

*Two children watch a a large anthill in Germany's Bavarian Forest.*

# Words to Know

abdomen (AB-duh-muhn) — the rear section of an insect's body

antennae (an-TEN-ee) — feelers on the head of an insect

cocoons (kuh-KOONZ) — coverings made from silky threads produced by the larvae of some insects and by certain other small animals to protect themselves or their eggs

colonies (KAH-luh-neez) — large groups of animals that live together

ecosystem (EE-koh-sis-tuhm) — all the living things in a place and their relation to their environment

fungus (FUHN-guhs) — a plantlike organism that has no leaves, flowers, roots, or chlorophyll and grows on other plants or decaying matter

habitats (HAB-uh-tats) — the places where an animal or a plant is usually found

insects (IN-sekts) — small animals with three pairs of legs, one or two pairs of wings, and three main parts to its body; insects have a hard outer skeleton and do not have a backbone

larva (LAR-vuh) — an insect at the stage of development between an egg and a pupa, when it looks like a worm

mate (MAYT) — join together to reproduce

molt (MOHLT) — to lose old fur, feathers, or skin so that new ones can grow

orders (OR-durz) — groups of related plants or animals that are bigger than a family but smaller than a class

predators (PREH-duh-turz) — animals that live by hunting other animals for food

prey (PRAY) — to hunt another animal for food

pupa (PYOO-puh) — an insect in an inactive stage of development between a larva and an adult

solitary (SAH-lih-ter-ee) — preferring to live alone

species (SPEE-sheez) — one of the groups into which animals and plants of the same genus are divided

thorax (THOR-aks) — the part of an insect's body between its head and its abdomen

NORTH

AMERICA

PACIFIC

ATLANTIC

OCEAN

SOUTH

AMERICA

Ant Range

ARCTIC OCEAN

EUROPE

ASIA

AFRICA

PACIFIC
OCEAN

OCEAN

INDIAN

OCEAN

AUSTRALIA

# Find Out More

**Books**

Gallagher, Debbie. *Ants*. New York: Marshall Cavendish Benchmark, 2012.

Gleason, Carrie. *Everything Insects*. Washington, DC: National Geographic, 2015.

Murawski, Darlyne, and Nancy Honovich. *Ultimate Bug-opedia: The Most Complete Bug Reference Ever*. Washington, DC: National Geographic, 2013.

Roesser, Marie. *Army Ants*. New York: Gareth Stevens Publishing, 2015.

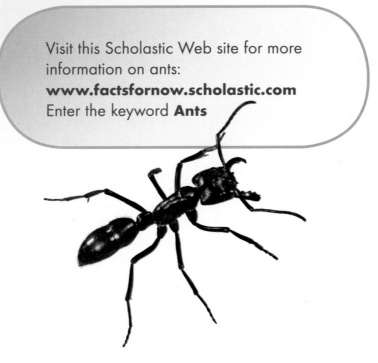

Visit this Scholastic Web site for more information on ants:
**www.factsfornow.scholastic.com**
Enter the keyword **Ants**

# Index

Page numbers in *italics* indicate a photograph or map.

# About the Author

Josh Gregory is the author of more than 90 books for kids. He has written about everything from animals to technology to history. A graduate of the University of Missouri-Columbia, he currently lives in Portland, Oregon.